TIPS *for Life*

READ IT.

LIVE IT.

PASS IT ON.

Read It.

Live It.

Pass It On.

Introduction by
Maria Shriver

TIPS
for Life

BRONZE BOW
PUBLISHING
bronzebowpublishing.com

Tips for Life

ISBN 978-1-59177-176-0

Published by Bronze Bow Publishing, Inc.
2600 E. 26th Street, Minneapolis, MN 55406

For additional copies of this book, call
Bronze Bow Publishing toll free at 866.724.8200
or go to www.bronzebowpublishing.com.

Cover/interior design by Koechel Peterson &
Associates, Inc., Minneapolis, Minnesota.
Cover photo: Magda Indigo
www.indigo2photography.co.uk

Printed in China

Foreword
MARIA SHRIVER

MORE THAN 150 OF THE WORLD'S
GREATEST VOICES, HEARTS AND MINDS
spoke at **The Women's Conference 2010**, the
nation's premier forum for inspiring, educating, and
empowering women. They ranged from global thought
leaders to corporate executives, healthcare experts to
spiritual guides, poets to social entrepreneurs, plus
activists, artists, actors and authors.

All of them have attained success and fulfillment in
their fields, but of course, they didn't start out that way.
On the bumpy, twisting road that led to where they are
today, these leaders got all the lumps and lessons that
shaped them into the Architects of Change they've
become.

We asked these inspirational people to give us some
of the bits of wisdom that helped them along the way—
Tips for Life.

In this collection, you'll find flashes of insight on the range of human experience—finding personal and professional fulfillment, being your own authentic self, learning from failure, negotiating love and relationships, taking care of your health and well-being. Some tips exhort you to live boldly and take risks. Others encourage you to take a breath and go easy.

I believe all of us can be Architects of Change in our own lives, in our communities, in the world. Wise words can be a beacon helping us get there—illuminating the path where we are and then guiding us to where we want to go.

I hope you turn to this book daily for meaning, motivation, and empowerment.

Read it.

Live it.

And then pass it on!

Maria Shriver

365 QUOTES
from more than 125 of the
world's greatest voices,
hearts and minds
with space to write
your personal reflections
on every spread.

1 JANUARY

You know those goals you've set for yourself, those dreams you've been waiting for the perfect time to live out? It's time.

Maria Shriver

First Lady of California

2 JANUARY

Dream big, think broadly about your life, and please make giving back to your community a part of that vision.

MICHELLE OBAMA

First Lady of the United States

3 JANUARY

What you believe has more power
than what you dream or wish or hope for.
You become what you believe.

Oprah Winfrey
Chairman, Harpo, Inc.
2010 Minerva Award® Recipient

4

Leave tracks. Just as others have been way-pavers for your good fortune, so you should aid those who will follow in your way.

The Honorable
Ruth Bader Ginsburg

Associate Justice, Supreme Court of the United States

5 JANUARY

It's never too late to set sail
and discover a new land
inside yourself.

Diane Sawyer

Anchor, ABC World News

6 JANUARY

Try to work at work worth doing.

Sandra Day O'Connor

Former Associate Justice,
Supreme Court of the United States,
2010 Minerva Award® Recipient

7 JANUARY

If you have compassion and commitment, you have everything you need to succeed.

Governor Arnold Schwarzenegger

Governor of California

A lot of things you can't repair with tales. Try love instead. Try self-love.

Mary Oliver

Pulitzer Prize-Winning & National Book Award-Winning Poet

9 JANUARY

Whether serving in your hometown
or on the other side of the world,
use your talents and energy to make
a better world. Wherever life leads you,
pursue the path of service and you will
find fulfillment beyond measure.

LAURA BUSH
Former First Lady of the United States

It's time to stop thumbing your way through life! To be an agent of change requires concentrated attention to a challenge.

Gail Sheehy

Best-Selling Author

11 JANUARY

It's time that YOU take control and own the power to control your financial destiny.

Suze Orman
America's Personal Finance Expert

12 JANUARY

Silence is underrated
and maybe even extinct.

Robert Redford

Actor, Activist, Entrepreneur

13 JANUARY

Get educated about what's in your food so you can heal yourself and your family while impacting change as an empowered consumer.

JILLIAN MICHAELS

Wellness Expert

No one has the timetable for your life. Consider the advice of others but follow your own inner alarm clock.

Martha Beck
Author, Life Coach

15 JANUARY

Despite our best science, if a heart doesn't have a reason to keep beating, it won't. Find meaning and purpose in your life. Nurture your relationships with loved ones. It's better than any medicine.

DR. MEHMET OZ

Host, The Dr. Oz Show

16 JANUARY

It's when you feel like everything is falling apart that you may learn and grow. So don't be scared to just be in that scary place.

Jane Fonda

Actor, Author, Fitness Advocate, Activist

17 JANUARY

Every woman has the power to change the world around them. It's instinctive for women to want to fix what is not right and change things for the better.

Paula Deen

Celebrity Cook, Entrepreneur, Author

The most important time
in your life is now.

Deepak Chopra

Founder, The Chopra Foundation

19 JANUARY

Serving with and for those in need,
you will answer the call to action
for social justice and you will change lives.
You will change the world.

Eunice Kennedy Shriver

Founder, Special Olympics,
2007 Minerva Lifetime Achievement Award® Recipient

20 JANUARY

The only time you must not fail is the last time you try.

PHIL KNIGHT

Co-Founder, Chairman, Nike Inc.

21 JANUARY

To be a credible leader, your words
and your actions must be aligned.
I can't just talk about what I believe.
I have to be involved.

Laysha Ward

President, Community Relations, Target Corporation

Frugality is not a word we hear often anymore. It means more than "don't spend money." To be frugal means to focus on what is important, and use resources wisely.

Jerry Brown
Attorney General of California,
2010 Democratic Candidate for Governor

23 JANUARY

It's time to let your hair down and enjoy the moment!

Giada De Laurentiis

*Celebrity Chef,
#1 New York Times' Best-Selling Cookbook Author*

24 JANUARY

Life is found in the dance
between your deepest desire
and your greatest fear.

TONY ROBBINS

Entrepreneur, Author,
Peak Performance Strategist

25 JANUARY

Find truth by living it.

Jessica Simpson
Singer, Actress, Entrepreneur

Success is best when it is shared.

Howard Schultz

*Chairman, President and
Chief Executive Officer,
Starbucks Coffee Company*

27 JANUARY

Give credit to others. Few major accomplishments in the working world are one-woman feats. Acknowledge, thank and promote the people who helped make it possible.

Larree Renda

Executive Vice President,
Chief Strategist and Administrative Officer,
Safeway, Inc.

Draw a big boundary between work and family. At the end of the day, yes, you have to pay the bills but you will never get back the family time you have now.

Cat Cora

First & Only Female Iron Chef, Executive Chef of Bon Appetit, President & Founder, Chefs for Humanity, Author

29 JANUARY

I don't make plans, because life is short and unpredictable— much like the weather!

Al Roker

Weather & Feature Reporter, NBC's The Today Show, President & CEO, Al Roker Entertainment

Give what you need the most.

Eve Ensler
Playwright, Performer, Activist

31 JANUARY

Speak up when it comes to your health concerns. If you don't ask, doctors won't tell. And if you don't tell, they won't ask.

DR. MARIE SAVARD

MD, Author of Ask Dr. Marie and Good Morning America Medical Contributor

Life is a series of choices
born into a world of agreements.
When you can see that, you are free.

Rosario Dawson

Actress, Co-Founder, Voto Latino

2 FEBRUARY

Every time we choose hope over despair, acceptance over intolerance, and optimism over negativity, we are doing our part to change the world.

Leeza Gibbons

Radio/TV Producer-Host,
Founder/Board Chair,
Leeza Gibbons Memory Foundation

Put on your favorite upbeat music and dance even when alone! Enhance the joy you were born with. Be fearless and celebrate the MOMENT.

Goldie Hawn

Actress

4 FEBRUARY

Success in life is about
showing up each day
with optimism and keen focus.

JAMES D. WHITE

*Chairman, President and
Chief Executive Officer, Jamba Juice*

Don't fear to ask.
They can't say "yes" unless you do.
And the worst they can do
is say "no."

Carolyn Blashek
Founder, Operation Gratitude,
2010 Minerva Award® Recipient

6 FEBRUARY

Awaken and give power
to your voice so you can thrive
and be heard in the world.

TRACEE ELLIS ROSS

Actress, Mentor, Teen Advocate

Life's too short.

Brian Williams

*Anchor and Managing Editor,
NBC Nightly News*

8 FEBRUARY

Be in the moment—
whether at work, with kids,
family or friends.
Be in the present and
enjoy what you're doing!

Susan Tousi

*General Manager of
Consumer Inkjet Systems,
Eastman Kodak Company*

"Women's issues" aren't of concern to women alone. These are human rights issues for us all. They challenge our consciences, not our chromosomes.

Nicholas Kristof

Columnist, New York Times

10 FEBRUARY

Appreciate that in today's open society no doors are closed to people willing to spend the effort needed to make dreams come true.

The Honorable Ruth Bader Ginsburg
Associate Justice, Supreme Court of the United States

11 FEBRUARY

The world needs women to redefine
what it means to be a person of power.

ELIZABETH LESSER

Co-Founder, Omega Institute

12 FEBRUARY

We need to start listening to other people, even if we don't agree with them— especially if we don't agree with them.

Gayle King

Editor at Large, O, The Oprah Magazine and Host of The Gayle King Show

Identify your own
unique strengths
and gifts.
Then act.

Rob Lowe

*Actor, Producer,
Entrepreneur*

14 FEBRUARY

Be inspired to continue
to work to transform
the lives of those in need.

Janice Mirikitani

*Executive Director of Glide Church
and President of the Glide Foundation,
Poet, 2005 Minerva Award® Recipient*

15 FEBRUARY

Have a vision for your future.
Start with a destination in mind.

LESLIE DANCE

*Director and Vice President
of Brand Marketing and
Communications,
Eastman Kodak Company*

16 FEBRUARY

Gratitude is the heart of friendship.

Louann Brizendine, M.D.

New York Times Best-Selling Author,
The Female Brain & The Male Brain

17 FEBRUARY

Getting older doesn't mean you forfeit all the other ages you've been. If I were to die today, it would be wrong to say I lost my life, for I have lived one.

LINDA ELLERBEE
Television Producer, Journalist, Best-Selling Author

18 FEBRUARY

Remember to be grateful
for all of the wonderful things
you have in your life.

Carol Kane

Actress

Don't fake it till you make it.
Be real, be transparent,
be authentic and be yourself.

Darren Hardy
Publisher and Editorial Director, SUCCESS

20 FEBRUARY

Listen to the inner voice that whispers, "You are on the right path," even as your enemies yell, "You are insane."

Claudia Julie Duque

Journalist, IWMF Courage in Journalism Award Winner 2010

21 FEBRUARY

If you can't change your circumstances,
change your perspective.

Anne Sweeney
Co-chair, Disney Media Networks,
President, Disney/ABC Television Group

22 FEBRUARY

To watch how lovingly your children parent their own children is to know profound achievement.

SALLY FIELD

Actress, Vital Voices Activist

23 FEBRUARY

We have a choice to
use the gift of our lives
to make the world
a better place.

Jane Goodall

*Founder, the Jane Goodall Institute
and UN Messenger of Peace,
2009 Minerva Award® Recipient*

24 FEBRUARY

Be kind when correcting others and always do so by putting yourself in their shoes.

Shinjo Ito
Founder of Shinnyo-en

25 FEBRUARY

Don't allow yourself to be defined by anyone—especially a man. Be your own person and be proud of who you are.

Lisa Ling

Journalist

26 FEBRUARY

Listen to stories from your relatives because their wisdom is unparalleled. Times change but the basic lessons of life remain the same.

BUDDY VALASTRO

Owner, Carlo's Bakery aka The Cake Boss

_____

_____

_____

_____

_____

_____

_____

27 FEBRUARY

Everything in life revolves
around only two things:
To choose to do something or
to choose not to do something.

Laila Ali

World Champion Athlete,
Television Personality, Mother

28 FEBRUARY

It is essential for women to do all we can to empower ourselves, to empower young women and to empower our communities through the services we provide.

LULA WASHINGTON

*Founder, Lula Washington
Contemporary Dance Foundation,
2004 Minerva Award® Recipient*

When playing with the boys, totally be a girl. Feminine attributes of intuition, flexibility and being a nurturer are winning business traits over ego and brawn.

Sonia Alleyne

Editorial Director, Black Enterprise

2 MARCH

We should live our life in such a way that someone will benefit from our stay here on earth.

Oral Lee Brown

*Founder, The Oral Lee Brown Foundation,
2010 Minerva Award® Recipient*

3 MARCH

Don't focus on the negative.

Jan Miller

President & Founder,
Dupree, Miller, & Associates

4 MARCH

The richness of your experiences throughout the years makes you who you are as an individual.

Maria Elena Salinas
Univision News Anchor

5 MARCH

Keep children interested in science and mathematics. The future of our nation requires it.

DR. SALLY RIDE

Director of the California Space Institute, Professor, Founder, The Sally Ride Science Center, 2006 Minerva Award® Recipient

6 MARCH

You cannot control every situation
or change in the workplace.
But you can control how you respond.

Lisa Stevens

EVP, Regional President,
California Regional Banking,
Wells Fargo & Company

7 MARCH

Be utterly, totally,
bravely truthful
and true to yourself.

Campbell Brown
Anchor

8 MARCH

Always be a beginner,
no matter how much
you think you know.

Peter Gallagher

Actor

9 MARCH

Learn something new and help someone else every day and the hard times will be a little easier.

CAROLINE KENNEDY
Vice Chair, New York City Fund for Public Schools

10 MARCH

You can live in the past
and may be miserable.
Or, you can live in the now
and make it better than
it ever was.

Billie Jean King
Co-Founder, World TeamTennis,
Wimbledon Champion,
Founder, Women's Sports Foundation
2009 Minerva Award® Recipient

11 MARCH

As a leader, you are the spark that lights the fire. Make your people face their fears and get moving.

CAROL BARTZ

CEO, Yahoo! Inc.

12 MARCH

Spend fun, joyful time with children...
they remind you what's REALLY important.

Crystal Ashby

*Vice President of Government and Public Affairs,
BP America Inc.*

You are the only thing that prevents yourself from feeling truly beautiful, valuable and worthwhile.

Katherine Schwarzenegger

Author, Rock What You've Got

14 MARCH

Be courageously bold
with yourself and shatter
all facades and delusions.
Invite your real life to begin.

Giselle Fernandez

President, F Squared Enterprises

15 MARCH

The only courage
you ever need is the
courage to live your
heart's desire.

Oprah Winfrey
Chairman, Harpo, Inc.
2010 Minerva Award® Recipient

16 MARCH

Take risks. You never move forward
if you stay in the same place.

MEGHAN McCAIN
Writer, Author

17 MARCH

Every time you deny who you are
you make another nick in your soul.

Dr. Susan Love

President, Dr. Susan Love Research Foundation

18 MARCH

One of the secrets of success is to accept change and be excited about it. See the possibilities, not the roadblocks.

William Margaritis

*Senior Vice President of
Global Communications
& Investor Relations, FedEx*

19 MARCH

Be willing to be the lone voice,
believe in the Power of One.
Never decide change is impossible.
Improbable is not the same thing
as impossible.

Caroline Aaron

Actress, Writer

20 MARCH

Plant a garden, even a window box
can produce great things. Herbs
such as basil, parsley, mint and thyme
can add tons of flavor to your food.

KIM BARNOUIN

Author, Skinny Bitch

21 MARCH

The way to roll with bad days
is to start every day by adding
another "thank you"
to your gratitude list.

Gail Sheehy
Best-Selling Author

22 MARCH

Time will never give you the window of a "perfect time." But it will always give you a window to be perfect at any "time."

DAYMOND JOHN

CEO, FUBU The Collection, Branding Expert, Author

Laugh as much as possible.

Kristin Perry

Plaintiff, Perry v. Schwarzenegger

24 MARCH

Never lose focus.
Never forget who you
want to serve and why.
Then the magic of
synergy takes over.

Agnes Stevens
Founder, School on Wheels,
2009 Minerva Award® Recipient

Own your brand and reputation. No one represents you better than you.

Nora Denzel

Senior Vice President and General Manager, Employee Management Solutions, Intuit Inc.

26 MARCH

We have everything we need,
right now, to help our kids
lead healthy lives.

Michelle Obama
First Lady of the United States

27 MARCH

First buy what you need, but stop denying the fun of buying what you love. Yes, budgets count, but the rationale, "Oh, where am I going to wear it?" is bogus. Buy it and the occasion will come.

HAL RUBENSTEIN
Fashion Director, InStyle Magazine

28 MARCH

Every time someone told
me I couldn't do it,
I took it as a challenge.

Alexandra Wentworth

Actress, Author, Host

Parenthood is the best excuse you'll ever find for becoming the person you want to be.

Teresa Delfin

Founder, Mountain Mama, Inc.

30 MARCH

If I am not a woman of hope, how can I ask others to have hope?

Sister Terry Dodge

Executive Director, Crossroads, Inc.,
2010 Minerva Award® Recipient

When you see an injustice,
it is your personal responsibility
to make a difference.

BETSY JOHNSON

*Educator, Community Organizer,
Diversity Advocate*

1 APRIL

Your words could be the wisdom that changes her life. Learn more by joining the Dove Movement for Self-Esteem.

Jess Weiner
*Global Ambassador for the
Dove Self-Esteem Fund*

2 APRIL

Change is inevitable. Take it from a couple who have made transformation their life's work.

DAVID AND DANIA MAAS

Quick Change Artists

3 APRIL

You hold the keys to your own kingdom.
Be fearlessly committed to your desires,
your beliefs, your soul and your true self.

Kristin Gibbs

General Manager, Consumer North America,
General Electric - Lighting Division, General Electric

Get your R.A.M. on!
"R" is for Realization,
when you REALIZE
it all begins with you.
Realize who you are
before you know
where to go.

Erin Brockovich
Environmental Activist, Author

5 APRIL

If I hadn't been myself all these years,
I'd have never become myself.

Christine Dahm

Vice President, Marketing,
Nestlé Prepared Foods Company

Overcoming challenges
and adversity in life
involves a moment
by moment decision
to not quit and
to keep going.

Kristina Ripatti
Retired LAPD Officer

7 APRIL

Every day is another chance to serve.
The opportunity to serve others
is one of life's greatest privileges.

HOLLY ROBINSON PEETE

Actress, Author, Activist, Philanthropist

I don't believe things "happen for a reason." But I firmly believe we can find meaning in the things that do happen.

Juju Chang

Good Morning America
News Anchor

9 APRIL

Envision it: A world with more love in it, simply because we want it that way.

Dr. Robert Epstein

Author, Professor

Turn your phone off
when you sit down
in the driver's seat.
It will still tell you
if someone called.

Jacy Good

FocusDriven Board Member

11 APRIL

Figuring out your life's purpose doesn't just happen. It takes hard work and no one but you can do it—but don't be afraid to ask for help along the way.

NANCY McFADDEN

Senior Vice President and Senior Advisor to the Chairman and CEO, PG&E Corporation

12 APRIL

The key to real, lasting change lies somewhere between what you know and what you do. It's what you think. To shift your behavior, start by transforming your thoughts.

Lisa Oz
Author

13 APRIL

What we love we must protect.
Our children cannot live without
a functioning biosphere. Therefore,
it's our job as parents to ensure
they have one.

SANDRA STEINGRABER

Acclaimed Ecologist, Author, Survivor

Be true to yourself and true to your cause and others will join you with equal intensity.

David Goldman

Devoted Father

15 APRIL

Opportunity is everywhere.
Give it life by your actions.

Sister Jennie Lechtenberg

*Founder and Executive Director
of Puente Learning Center,
2005 Minerva Award® Recipient*

16 APRIL

Accept yourself
so you can expect
more from yourself.

Gretchen Rubin

Writer, The Happiness Project

17 APRIL

We all deserve the opportunity
to be the best that we can be.
This is only accomplished by giving
or receiving loving assistance.
Do at least one.

Rafer Johnson

U.S. Olympian and Founder,
Special Olympics Southern California

18 APRIL

Believe in yourself.

TAMI ERWIN

President, West Area,
Verizon Wireless

19 APRIL

Incredible mothering means encouraging, supporting and loving your children during their transformation into the people they need to be.

Mary Ann Wasil Nilan

Author, A Diary of Healing;
Executive Director & Founder,
The Get In Touch Foundation;
2009 Day of Transformation
Book Writing Contest Winner

It's never too late to start anything.
There is never a "right" time.
You just have to jump in and start.

Rita Wilson
Actress, Producer

21 APRIL

Love and Live now—
the moments are passing
and you will not
get that time back.

Azure Antoinette

Poet, Spoken Word Artist

22 APRIL

Take time each day to make sure your family knows you love them "bigger than the world." Say it as often as you can.

CAT CORA

First & Only Female Iron Chef, Executive Chef of Bon Appetit, President & Founder, Chefs for Humanity, Author

23 APRIL

Life is too short
to get too flustered.

The Most Rev.
Dr. Katharine Jefferts Schori

Presiding Bishop and Primate,
The Episcopal Church

24

We all have an obligation to give back to the universe. Serving others and making a difference in someone's life will fulfill you more than serving yourself.

RODNEY PEETE

Sports Star, TV/Radio Personality, Author, Philanthropist

25 APRIL

Everyone's broken,
everyone's perfect.
There's no shame in any of it.

Natasha Lyonne

Actress

Business-savvy starts with having people-savvy. Being authentic makes you more interesting, unique and real. Amplify your true personality and pair it with your expertise.

Lloyd Boston
Television Host, Style Expert and Best-Selling Author

27 APRIL

A good friendship is like a seesaw: Sometimes you take and sometimes you give, but there is balance between the two of you in the long run.

Alice Domar

Director, Domar Center for Mind/Body Health,
Co-Author, Live a Little, Expert, BeWell.com

Make your life experience
be a positive force.
Be that advocate to help
others help themselves.

Jennie Hernandez Gin

*Co-Founder, WEAVE
(Women Escaping a
Violent Environment),
2008 Minerva Award® Recipient*

29 APRIL

Smart girls think about money.
Do something daily to profit
from your passion and potential.

TORY JOHNSON

CEO, Women For Hire;
Workplace Contributor,
Good Morning America

If you can hit the elliptical,
while reading a book,
with your laundry running,
as you chat with a friend,
you can DEFINITELY
tackle your finances.

Alexa von Tobel

Founder, CEO, LearnVest Inc.

1 MAY

You've got to change
the way you think
in order to change
the way you feel.

Robin Roberts
*Co-Anchor, ABC's
Good Morning America*

As women, we don't have to choose between being a great mother and fulfilling our dreams of building a business. We can do both beautifully.

Soleil Moon Frye

Actress, Director, Screenwriter, Entrepreneur

3 MAY

When all looks hopeless—
fight even harder.

DEBORAH ROBERTS
ABC News Correspondent

Believe in yourself.
Trust the process.
Change forever.

Bob Harper
TV Personality

5 MAY

Dare to make yourself an example
of the best of man's humanity to man
and watch the world change around you.

LUONG UNG

Activist, Author, Lecturer

6 MAY

Take time each day
to practice the act
of gratitude. It will
bring you greater peace.

Laura Ling

Journalist

7 MAY

Know that inside every successful person
is someone who experienced failure
but refused to let it define them,
picked themselves up and kept going.

Judy Woodruff
Senior Correspondent, The PBS NewsHour

8 MAY

To achieve your dreams,
you must have your heart
in what you're doing.
You can touch people's lives
with genuine compassion.
The most powerful leadership
is to lead by the example
of your own life.

Helen Waukazoo

*CEO, Friendship House Association
of American Indians, Inc.,
2009 Minerva Award® Recipient*

9 MAY

You know that voice
that keeps saying
"can't, won't, shouldn't,"
and "too late?"
Tell it to shut up.

Jeannie Mai
Host, How Do I Look?
The Style Network

10 MAY

Only if you are ready to change yourself can you be ready to change the world.

EDIT SCHLAFFER

Founder, Women without Borders,
SAVE - Sisters Against Violent Extremism

11 MAY

A wish changes nothing.
A decision changes everything.
Make that decision and
YOU WILL SUCCEED!

Jake Steinfeld

Chairman and CEO of Body by Jake Global

What are you waiting for?
This isn't a dress rehearsal.
There are no do-overs.

Anne Mulcahy
Former Chairman and CEO,
Xerox Corporation

13 MAY

Be authentic. It's so much easier
to be who you are 100 percent
of the time than be something else—
even for a minute.

Blair Christie

Senior Vice President,
Corporate Communications, Cisco

14 MAY

You will never be younger or more beautiful than you are right now.

SANDRA STIER

Plaintiff, Perry v. Schwarzenegger

15 MAY

Love yourself. Give yourself time to be with the people, places and things you love most.

Donna Karan
Fashion Icon, Philanthropist

16 MAY

For Paul the Apostle everything changed in a moment on the road to Damascus. Have you had your road to Damascus moment yet? Is it time?

LAVERN VIVIO

Christian Speaker and Radio Personality

17 MAY

Social change is like a standing ovation— at first only a few may stand up, then more, then everyone. Don't be afraid to stand up and clap for what is right. Others will follow eventually.

Molly Melching

Executive Director, Tostan

18 MAY

Be the mentor you wish you'd had.

Graciela Meibar
Vice President Global Diversity, Mattel, Inc.

19 MAY

You can lead a man to the trough but you can't make him drink. But when you create a thirst, he will want to drink.

Sweet Alice Harris

Founder and Executive Director of Parents of Watts, 2007 Minerva Award® Recipient

20 MAY

If we do our jobs right as mothers, our daughters will grow from little girls into young ladies then raucous women.

Caroline Aaron

Actress, Writer

21 MAY

The most important thing you can do
is make a decision. It's better to make
a mistake that can be quickly corrected
than let the opportunity slip away.

DR. MEHMET OZ

Host, The Dr. Oz Show

You define your own life.
Don't let other people
write your script.

Oprah Winfrey

Chairman, Harpo, Inc.,
2010 Minerva Award® Recipient

23 MAY

Sometimes you have to be
the one to stand up and say,
"The emperor has no clothes!"

Dr. Susan Love
President, Dr. Susan Love
Research Foundation

Tomorrow has just begun.

Caroline Kennedy

Vice Chair, New York City Fund for Public Schools

25 MAY

Share your talents with a charity as a volunteer. The skills that you've honed in the workplace can make a tremendous impact in your community.

LARREE RENDA

Executive Vice President, Chief Strategist and Administrative Officer, Safeway, Inc.

Reverse the Golden Rule for Life.
Do first for yourself what you have
always done first for others.

Dr. Marie Savard

*MD, Author of Ask Dr. Marie
and Good Morning America
Medical Contributor*

27 MAY

Preparation = Confidence.

LAILA ALI
World Champion Athlete,
Television Personality, Mother

28

We are accustomed to hearing "pay yourself first" when it comes to managing our finances. We need to do the same thing with our bodies and our spirits so we can manage our emotions and our health.

Leeza Gibbons

Radio/TV Producer-Host, Founder/Board Chair, Leeza Gibbons Memory Foundation

29 MAY

Stay open. Have faith in yourself. Trust in the significance of your life and the purpose of your passion.

Jillian Michaels

Wellness Expert

30 MAY

Time is the most valuable currency in the world. Those who squander it will create depreciating assets for their remaining years. Those that value it will benefit greatly from its dividends.

Daymond John

CEO, FUBU The Collection, Branding Expert, Author

31 MAY

Assimilation does not
necessarily mean leaving
behind your culture
but actually embracing
a new one.

Maria Elena Salinas
Univision News Anchor

1 JUNE

No matter how good you are
and how well you're performing,
there's always something
you can learn from someone else.

LISA STEVENS

EVP, Regional President,
California Regional Banking,
Wells Fargo & Company

2 JUNE

They say time goes.
They're wrong.
Time stays. We go.

Linda Ellerbee

Television Producer,
Journalist, Best-Selling Author

3 JUNE

Every single one of us is born
with a canvas: our lives.
Every single one of us can
create a masterpiece with
the life that we've been given.

Maria Shriver
First Lady of California

4 JUNE

Compassion and confidence are a powerful combination for a leader.

Blair Christie

Senior Vice President,
Corporate Communications, Cisco

5 JUNE

If you are desperate to change
the life you live, identify the story
you tell yourself about who you are
and change it to a story that
makes you worthy of the dream!

GISELLE FERNANDEZ

President, F Squared Enterprises

6 JUNE

Eat ice cream with your kids
once a week in the summertime
and don't feel guilty about it.

Campbell Brown

Anchor

Helping people is harder than it looks. But our efforts to empower others also empower ourselves.

NICHOLAS KRISTOF

Columnist, New York Times

8 JUNE

Always have hope.

Laura Ling

Journalist

9 JUNE

Do not wait to live.
Own what you know in your heart.
The day you own it and act on it,
the world opens up in a whole new way!

Giselle Fernandez
President, F Squared Enterprises

10 JUNE

Never stop learning
from your children.
I learn more from mine
the older they get.

Gayle King

*Editor at Large, O, The Oprah Magazine
and Host of The Gayle King Show*

The more we examine ourselves
and learn from our mistakes,
the clearer our future becomes.

Shinjo Ito
Founder of Shinnyo-en

12 JUNE

Change doesn't
happen overnight.
It starts with the desire,
then one small step
in the right direction.

PAULA DEEN

*Celebrity Cook,
Entrepreneur, Author*

13 JUNE

When I hit a wall and feel overburdened,
I think of my 78-year-old mother who
still volunteers for friends and family.
This puts things in perspective.

Maureen Pennington

Senior Nurse Executive,
U.S. Naval Medical Center San Diego,
2007 Minerva Award® Recipient

14 JUNE

Strive for a world in which daughters
are cherished fully as much as sons.

The Honorable Ruth Bader Ginsburg
Associate Justice, Supreme Court of the United States

15 JUNE

Don't do for a woman what she is capable of doing for herself. Teach her how to do it.

Sister Terry Dodge

Executive Director, Crossroads, Inc.
2010 Minerva Award® Recipient

16 JUNE

You don't have to figure everything out.
Relax into the mystery of being alive.

ELIZABETH LESSER

Co-Founder, Omega Institute

With every breath we change.
Transformation is a way of life.
Why not make it an art form?
We did!

David and Dania Maas
Quick Change Artists

18 JUNE

Always put your needs on your own to-do list. When you wake up, think of one nice thing you can do for yourself that day.

ALICE DOMAR

Director, Domar Center for Mind/Body Health,
Co-Author, Live a Little,
Expert, BeWell.com

Tell yourself how truly beautiful you are at least once a day. You deserve it!

Katherine Schwarzenegger

Author, Rock What You've Got

20 JUNE

Discover, accept, love
and take responsibility
for who you really are!

Tracee Ellis Ross
Actress, Mentor, Teen Advocate

Your thoughts create your life.
You are what you think.

Jan Miller

President & Founder,
Dupree, Miller, & Associates

22 JUNE

Don't succumb to "prison thinking," setting limitations for yourself that hold you back.

William Margaritis
Senior Vice President
of Global Communications
& Investor Relations, FedEx

The best tools in working for social change
are respect, optimism and perseverance.

MOLLY MELCHING

Executive Director, Tostan

24 JUNE

There is no end to a
woman's growth—
make personal time
each day for self-reflection
and personal enhancement.

Cat Cora

First & Only Female Iron Chef,
Executive Chef of Bon Appetit,
President & Founder,
Chefs for Humanity, Author

They say there is life after breast cancer.
I say there is life right in the middle
of breast cancer. I've never been more alive!

Mary Ann Wasil Nilan

Author, A Diary of Healing;
Executive Director & Founder, The Get In Touch Foundation;
2009 Day of Transformation Book Writing Contest Winner

26 JUNE

Get your RAM on!
The "A" is for Assessment.
Take stock, not in what
you have but who you are.
If your appraisal comes in
at anything less than priceless,
make some changes!

Erin Brockovich

Environmental Activist, Author

27 JUNE

Dream big, take small
positive actions each day
and write down the plan.

JAMES D. WHITE

*Chairman, President and
Chief Executive Officer, Jamba Juice*

28 JUNE

When you envision a goal,
there is always a way
to accomplish the mission.

Carolyn Blashek
Founder, Operation Gratitude,
2010 Minerva Award® Recipient

29 JUNE

I've only watched my feet as I've moved through life and am amazed to see the distance I've traveled.

SALLY FIELD

Actress, Vital Voices Activist

30 JUNE

Be charitable—generosity will improve your life.

Leslie Dance

Director and Vice President of Brand Marketing and Communications, Eastman Kodak Company

1 JULY

Understanding, defining
and believing what success
means to you is the only way
for you to be successful.

Rodney Peete
*Sports Star, TV/Radio Personality,
Author, Philanthropist*

2 JULY

Take a moment every day simply to be thankful that you are alive and never forget that life is still really good despite the sad parts.

Jacy Good

FocusDriven Board Member

Don't assume you must struggle alone. There's a lot of grace and comfort in asking for help.

Tory Johnson

CEO, Women For Hire;
Workplace Contributor,
Good Morning America

4 JULY

Share and give back
in the areas most
important to you.
Take action. Don't
think about it—do it.

DONNA KARAN

Fashion Icon, Philanthropist

Surround yourself with color—
colorful flowers, colorful clothing,
colorful people. It can make
you feel so good.

Gayle King

*Editor at Large, O, The Oprah Magazine
and Host of The Gayle King Show*

6 JULY

Help a girl in your life
develop a positive
relationship with beauty.
You can empower her
to reach her full potential.

Kathy O'Brien
*Vice President Unilever
Personal Care*

Remember to ask for help.
We are never alone.
Children work to please.
Adults want to feel needed.
Ask for help.

Anita DeFrantz

President of the LA84 Foundation,
2005 Minerva Award® Recipient

8 JULY

Tune out the naysayers
and listen to your heart.

GOVERNOR ARNOLD SCHWARZENEGGER

Governor of California

There are many things
we can live without
but a sense of humor
is not one of them!

Judy Woodruff
Senior Correspondent,
The PBS NewsHour

10 JULY

When you're making decisions, do it from a place of hope, not fear. Hope is oxygen for your soul.

SANDRA STIER

Plaintiff, Perry v. Schwarzenegger

If you aren't scared, then you aren't learning anything new.

Anne Sweeney

Co-chair, Disney Media Networks,
President, Disney/ABC Television Group

12 JULY

Rid your world of all wars,
crimes, scandals, gossip
and corruption in an instant:
Turn off your TV, radio and
newspaper subscription.

Darren Hardy
Publisher and Editorial Director, SUCCESS

13 JULY

Ask yourself if you're
seeking change
or approval.

Eve Ensler

Playwright, Performer, Activist

14 JULY

I'm grateful for my mistakes
because I learned from them.
If I didn't, I'd be in Belleview.

Alexandra Wentworth

Actress, Author, Host

15 JULY

I never understood how parenting didn't come with a manual. I don't need a license for this?

SOLEIL MOON FRYE

Actress, Director, Screenwriter, Entrepreneur

16 JULY

Put at least as much effort into your relationships as your career. Your family and friends can be your source of greatest strength.

Anne Mulcahy

*Former Chairman and CEO,
Xerox Corporation*

17 JULY

The purpose of life is to create happiness around you now.

Deepak Chopra
Founder, The Chopra Foundation

18 JULY

The person you find most challenging has a gift for you— will you try to discover it?

The Most Rev. Dr. Katharine Jefferts Schori

Presiding Bishop and Primate, The Episcopal Church

19 JULY

No hard work ever goes to waste—
even if it doesn't bear fruit to where
you want it. It will either help you
grow or be the start of an archive
of knowledge you can pull from
at any time.

LLOYD BOSTON

*Television Host, Style Expert
and Best-Selling Author*

20 JULY

Keep a gratitude journal to note what you are grateful for. Expressing gratitude has profoundly proven to boost your happiness level and change your state of mind.

Goldie Hawn

Actress

21 JULY

You can choose what you do but you can't choose what you like to do.

GRETCHEN RUBIN

Writer, The Happiness Project

22 JULY

Don't wait. You are ready now! Tomorrow you will be wiser— and realize that you really should have started yesterday.

Sonia Alleyne

Editorial Director, Black Enterprise

In the end, truth matters.

Nancy McFadden

*Senior Vice President and Senior Advisor
to the Chairman and CEO, PG&E Corporation*

24 JULY

Don't just do what you can do.
Do what ONLY you can do.

Rob Lowe

Actor, Producer, Entrepreneur

To help a child, give him or her a job.

To free a child, give him or her an education.

I want all the children to be free.

Oral Lee Brown

Founder, The Oral Lee Brown Foundation,
2010 Minerva Award® Recipient

26 JULY

For children, books can be an unending source of information about who they are and who they can become. Together we can fill library shelves with books and children's lives with possibility.

LAURA BUSH

Former First Lady of the United States

27 JULY

When you're
expecting adventure,
it will find you.

Teresa Delfìn

Founder, Mountain Mama, Inc.

28 JULY

Give. Give Big. Give Bountifully.
Give back not because you
have to but because you get to.

Holly Robinson Peete

Actress, Author, Activist, Philanthropist

Never be passive about love.

Dr. Robert Epstein

Author, Professor

30 JULY

Life is full of choices. Make choices that will make your journey in life the best that it can be.

BETSY JOHNSON

Educator, Community Organizer, Diversity Advocate

31 JULY

Too often, we spend our days thinking about what we don't have rather than what we do have. Be grateful every day.

Lisa Ling
Journalist

1 AUGUST

If you love what you do,
you won't mind
the journey to success.

JEANNIE MAI

Host, How Do I Look?
The Style Network

Prepare today for the challenges you will face tomorrow.

Kristina Ripatti

Retired LAPD Officer

3 AUGUST

Give what you do 100 percent.
You should feel great. If you don't,
do something else.

Buddy Valastro
Owner, Carlo's Bakery aka The Cake Boss

Read a poem each day. The poems I memorized as a child still calm me before an important board meeting.

Christy Porter

Founder and Executive Director of Hidden Harvest, 2007 Minerva Award® Recipient

5 AUGUST

The Buddha knew nothing until
he walked out into the world.
Mary knew nothing until
she walked out into the world.

Mary Oliver
*Pulitzer Prize-Winning & National
Book Award-Winning Poet*

Negative self-talk doesn't help at all.

Natasha Lyonne

Actress

7 AUGUST

Fake confidence if you have to—
even you will be convinced.

Deborah Roberts

ABC News Correspondent

8 AUGUST

The one thing we have
absolute control over
is our internal world.
We decide what things
mean and what to do
about them.

Tony Robbins
*Entrepreneur, Author,
Peak Performance Strategist*

9 AUGUST

When you know it's time for action, act. When you feel it's time to rest, rest. Not resting is as harmful as not acting.

Martha Beck

Author/Life Coach

You are good enough already.

LOUANN BRIZENDINE, M.D.

New York Times Best-Selling Author,
The Female Brain & The Male Brain

11 AUGUST

It's time to celebrate you:
unique, wonderful you.
Do that each and every day.

Graciela Meibar
Vice President Global Diversity, Mattel, Inc.

12

It's Time that you say NO
out of LOVE versus YES
out of fear.

SUZE ORMAN
America's Personal Finance Expert

13 AUGUST

Acknowledge your power
as an alternative female diplomat
and you will change the world.

Edit Schlaffer

Founder, Women without Borders,
SAVE - Sisters Against Violent Extremism

14 AUGUST

Progress can only be made
by joining a coalition of WE.

Gail Sheehy
Best-Selling Author

15 AUGUST

The world let's YOU be what YOU make them believe YOU are!

Jake Steinfeld

Chairman and CEO of Body by Jake Global

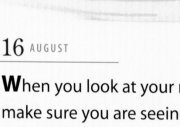

16 AUGUST

When you look at your reflection
make sure you are seeing through
your own eyes.

Jessica Simpson
Singer, Actress, Entrepreneur

17 AUGUST

When you stumble, it's best
to get up, put one foot in front of
the other, and keep moving forward.

BILLIE JEAN KING

Co-Founder, World TeamTennis,
TWimbledon Champion,
Founder, Women's Sports Foundation
2009 Minerva Award® Recipient

Learn to live without regrets and stop striving for perfection—you may be missing all the fun stuff in between!

Crystal Ashby

Vice President of Government and Public Affairs, BP America Inc.

19 AUGUST

Live with gratitude.

Juju Chang

Good Morning America News Anchor

20 AUGUST

I have created a life by stepping out of the box of people's limitations. I call it zigging when others are zagging.

Oprah Winfrey

Chairman, Harpo, Inc.,
2010 Minerva Award® Recipient

21 AUGUST

Credibility is the sweet reward of speaking truth to power.

CLAUDIA JULIE DUQUE

Journalist, IWMF Courage in Journalism Award Winner 2010

22 AUGUST

Before you set out to accomplish something, make absolutely sure you are right. Then give it all you have.

David Goldman
Devoted Father

23 AUGUST

In the face of incredible struggles,
refuse to be defined by the hardships
or adversities. Instead, what defines
you is your perseverance.

MICHELLE OBAMA

First Lady of the United States

24 AUGUST

If a job is worth doing,
it is worth doing right.

Tami Erwin

President, West Area, Verizon Wireless

25 AUGUST

Help others help themselves. Always try to make "more room at the inn" to help turn more lives around.

Mimi Silbert

*Founder, President and CEO,
Delancey Street Foundation,
2004 Minerva Award® Recipient*

26 AUGUST

Smile—even when you don't feel like it. It changes the neural pathways in your brain. Plus, you'll look better.

Jane Fonda

Actor, Author, Fitness Advocate, Activist

27 AUGUST

While most of what happens to us is outside of our control, the one thing we actually determine is how we choose to respond to life's events.

Lisa Oz

Author

You don't have to try to impress your kids. If they're not getting what they need from you, they will let you know.

AL ROKER

Weather & Feature Reporter,
NBC's The Today Show,
President & CEO,
Al Roker Entertainment

29 AUGUST

Invest in people and we will all bear witness.

Luong Ung

Activist, Author, Lecturer

30 AUGUST

Every child deserves a high quality education—regardless of race or class—to ensure they graduate from high school ready for college and a career.

Laysha Ward
President, Community Relations, Target Corporation

31 AUGUST

It's time to bake some goodies
and share them with your neighbors.

Giada De Laurentiis

Celebrity Chef, #1 New York Times'
Best-Selling Cookbook Author

1 SEPTEMBER

When it comes to change, don't just preach it. You need to role-model the behavior you want others to adopt.

CAROL BARTZ

CEO, Yahoo! Inc.

2 SEPTEMBER

Nobody knows anything, which gives each of us good reason to keep showing up.

Peter Gallagher
Actor

3 SEPTEMBER

Having children makes you realize how quickly time does pass. Every moment with your children or loved ones must be savored and never taken for granted.

RITA WILSON

Actress, Producer

4 SEPTEMBER

Choose a mentor, someone who will support your goals and be an advocate for you. Having a source of inspiration inspires greatness.

Christine Dahm

*Vice President, Marketing,
Nestlé Prepared Foods Company*

5 SEPTEMBER

You can't can't do anything.

Bob Harper
TV Personality

_____

_____

_____

_____

_____

_____

_____

_____

_____

6 SEPTEMBER

Slow down.

Kristin Perry

Plaintiff, Perry v. Schwarzenegger

When life is threatened, the need for more data isn't an excuse to do nothing. Act on what you know. That's called the "Precautionary Principle."

Sandra Steingraber
Acclaimed Ecologist, Author, Survivor

8 SEPTEMBER

The efforts of one individual
can touch thousands of women.

DR. HELENE BROWN

*Co-Chair, Futures Initiative
of the American Cancer Society,
2004 Minerva Award® Recipient*

Learn to ask for what you want. Don't wait for someone to read your mind.

Nora Denzel

Senior Vice President and General Manager, Employee Management Solutions, Intuit Inc.

10 SEPTEMBER

We must work hard, but not be so busy that no time is left to love and walk hand-in-hand with your family.

Rafer Johnson

U.S. Olympian and Founder,
Special Olympics Southern California

Take it one moment at a time,
sometimes a day is too much.

Azure Antoinette

Poet, Spoken Word Artist

12 SEPTEMBER

Pay someone a compliment today.
It will make you feel good and brighten
the person's day.

Katherine Schwarzenegger

Author, Rock What You've Got

Are you at peace with this moment
or at war with what is happening?
Take stock of yourself right now.
Call a truce.

Elizabeth Lesser

Co-Founder, Omega Institute

14 SEPTEMBER

Take five minutes in the morning and evening to quiet your mind. Find a quiet space and focus on your breath. Notice your thoughts and let them fly away. Always return to your breath. This has proven to reduce stress and enhance your brain's potential. Stress steals our happiness!

GOLDIE HAWN

Actress

15 SEPTEMBER

Knowledge is power so never stop learning.
Know your business and industry inside
and out to determine where you can make
the biggest impact.

Larree Renda

Executive Vice President,
Chief Strategist and Administrative Officer, Safeway, Inc.

16 SEPTEMBER

The best way to tell
the future is to create it.

Rosario Dawson

*Actress, Co-Founder,
Voto Latino*

17 SEPTEMBER

Coincidence is when God chooses to remain anonymous.

Carolyn Blashek

Founder, Operation Gratitude,
2010 Minerva Award® Recipient

18 SEPTEMBER

The best way to create your future
is to make the right choices now.

Deepak Chopra
Founder, The Chopra Foundation

19 SEPTEMBER

Maybe it's time to stop achieving and start receiving. The biggest victory may be in our ability to feel gratitude, to receive the gifts of the universe.

LEEZA GIBBONS

Radio/TV Producer-Host, Founder/Board Chair, Leeza Gibbons Memory Foundation

20 SEPTEMBER

Before making any decision,
ask yourself "Why?" and, then,
"Why not?" to manage impulsiveness
and make transformational choices.

Jillian Michaels

Wellness Expert

21 SEPTEMBER

Get comfortable with being uncomfortable,
you'll be amazed at what you can accomplish.

Nora Denzel

Senior Vice President and General Manager,
Employee Management Solutions, Intuit Inc.

22 SEPTEMBER

Show up, pay attention, tell the truth, and leave the results to God.

**The Most Rev.
Dr. Katharine Jefferts Schori**

Presiding Bishop and Primate, The Episcopal Church

23 SEPTEMBER

Change is important.
Without it how can one imagine
what you could become?

David and Dania Maas
Quick Change Artists

24 SEPTEMBER

A lifetime of good sleep
is the secret potion our bodies
crave but rarely receive.

DR. MARIE SAVARD

MD, *Author of Ask Dr. Marie and*
Good Morning America Medical Contributor

25 SEPTEMBER

A hero is a person who doesn't count the cost of sacrifice in time, money and convenience to bring joy and laughter and hope to the infants and children who are hungry, to women who are overpowered or to families who are ignored.

Eunice Kennedy Shriver

Founder, Special Olympics,
2007 Minerva Lifetime Achievement Award® Recipient

26 SEPTEMBER

What does your best day look like?
Live a piece of it every day.

Juju Chang

Good Morning America News Anchor

27 SEPTEMBER

It's Time that you trust yourself
more than you trust others.

Suze Orman
America's Personal Finance Expert

28 SEPTEMBER

Focus on "I will" instead of "I will try."
Say to yourself, "I can do this, I WILL do this."
What you tell yourself is what will happen.

William Margaritis

*Senior Vice President of Global Communications
& Investor Relations, FedEx*

29 SEPTEMBER

When you see a problem in your world, seek the solution. Becoming an Architect of Change is as simple as that.

Maria Shriver
First Lady of California

30 SEPTEMBER

Remember to validate the efforts of your peers.

IVELISE MARKOVITS

Founder and CEO, Penny Lane Centers,
2008 Minerva Award® Recipient

1 OCTOBER

I've never believed in keeping my eye on the prize. If you do, you miss the whole game.

Alexandra Wentworth

Actress, Author, Host

2 OCTOBER

By giving women the tools they need to succeed—such as access to education and healthcare—they not only improve the well-being of their own families, but the stability of their communities.

Laura Bush
Former First Lady of the United States

3 OCTOBER

The first half of your life is spent meticulously learning the rules of the game so you can spend the second half of your life successfully breaking them.

Dr. Mehmet Oz

Host, The Dr. Oz Show

4 OCTOBER

Personally and professionally,
visualize yourself reaching your goals.
If you can see it, you can achieve it!

BLAIR CHRISTIE

Senior Vice President, Corporate Communications, Cisco

5 OCTOBER

God gave us life, what are we
willing to give him in return?

Oral Lee Brown
*Founder, The Oral Lee Brown Foundation,
2010 Minerva Award® Recipient*

6 OCTOBER

Nurture someone's desire
to make things better and watch
tomorrow's leader blossom.

PAULA DEEN

Celebrity Cook, Entrepreneur, Author

7 OCTOBER

Being late is rarely cute,
sometimes forgivable, always rude.

Hal Rubenstein

Fashion Director, InStyle Magazine

8 OCTOBER

If you walk out into the world
in anger or self-centeredness,
even the sparrows will scatter.

Mary Oliver
Pulitzer Prize-Winning & National Book Award-Winning Poet

"**M**" is for Motivation. To find success you must get motivated. It's the fuel that keeps you moving.

Erin Brockovich

Environmental Activist, Author

10 OCTOBER

The best ideas always come after you have explored tons of so-so ideas. Just when you think you have created a bunch of fresh concepts, push yourself to create the same amount more and you'll hit the big idea!

Lloyd Boston
Television Host, Style Expert and Best-Selling Author

Enjoy life. Slow down. Laugh.

RITA WILSON

Actress, Producer

12 OCTOBER

If you're feeling miserable, force yourself to smile broadly, holding your goofy grin at least 10 seconds. When you relax your face, you'll actually feel happier.

Sandra Stier

Plaintiff, Perry v. Schwarzenegger

13 OCTOBER

There are no regrets if you do your best.

Laura Ling

Journalist

14 OCTOBER

Consider yoga. Find the right style for you. Yoga is a way of life, connecting the mind, body and spirit. It's your daily calm in the chaos.

Donna Karan

Fashion Icon, Philanthropist

15 OCTOBER

You should feel guilty after lying
or infidelity, not after eating a cupcake.

GAYLE KING

*Editor at Large, O, The Oprah Magazine
and Host of The Gayle King Show*

16 OCTOBER

Love is much too important
to be left to chance.

Dr. Robert Epstein
Author, Professor

Learn to love yourself,
all of yourself—the good,
the imperfect, the endearing.
It reminds you to embrace
the foibles of others with grace.

CRYSTAL ASHBY

*Vice President of Government and
Public Affairs, BP America Inc.*

18 OCTOBER

Turn off the TV and read.

Campbell Brown

Anchor

19 OCTOBER

Plan theme night dinners by
making dishes from other countries.
It will introduce you to great new flavors
and change up your cooking routine.

Kim Barnouin
Author, Skinny Bitch

20 OCTOBER

Labels create barriers that say
you are different, you are
not like me. I work with women,
not drug addicts, not parolees,
not ex-felons. I work with women.

Sister Terry Dodge

Executive Director, Crossroads, Inc.
2010 Minerva Award® Recipient

21 OCTOBER

Good leadership is all about
developing good follower-ship.
In today's world, more than ever.

Anne Mulcahy
Former Chairman and CEO,
Xerox Corporation

22 OCTOBER

Being able to help others
is a great gift.

GLORIA STEINEM

*Author and Creator, the Ms. Foundation,
2008 Minerva Award® Recipient*

23 OCTOBER

Failure is just a pit stop on the road to success. Stop, adjust and keep it movin'.

Holly Robinson Peete

Actress, Author, Activist, Philanthropist

24 OCTOBER

Visualize your goals. Trust yourself.
And never, ever, be afraid to fail.

Governor Arnold Schwarzenegger
Governor of California

My great-grandma Hattie,
who lived to be 105, always said,
"There are a few things in life
worth fighting for: Family, friends,
faith, freedom and an education."

Laysha Ward

President, Community Relations,
Target Corporation

26 OCTOBER

I won't be inspired until I believe
I can be the one who inspires.

JESSICA SIMPSON

Singer, Actress, Entrepreneur

Women need to know their bodies better than their mothers ever did, or their grandmothers would ever approve of.

Mary Ann Wasil Nilan

Author, A Diary of Healing;
Executive Director & Founder, The Get In Touch Foundation;
2009 Day of Transformation Book Writing Contest Winner

28 OCTOBER

If you and your partner have nothing to talk about at dinner, it's unlikely you'll have much to express later that night. If you want a more interesting sex-life, start with the life part.

LISA OZ

Author

Enjoy today.
It is not yesterday
or tomorrow.

Betsy Johnson

*Educator, Community Organizer,
Diversity Advocate*

30

Dove believes beauty should be
a source of confidence, not anxiety.
Help us make this vision a reality by
joining the Dove Movement for Self-Esteem.

Kathy O'Brien
Vice President Unilever Personal Care

Think before you tweet
(what you place on the internet lives
in the universe and can't be undone).

Meghan McCain

Writer, Author

1 NOVEMBER

Think of your children and grandchildren to come. Do your part to make society as you would want it to be for them.

The Honorable Ruth Bader Ginsburg

Associate Justice, Supreme Court of the United States

2 NOVEMBER

Forgive. Don't condone, but forgive
and move on. It's the very best revenge.

SALLY FIELD

Actress, Vital Voices Activist

3 NOVEMBER

An excuse will shatter a dream every single time.

Bob Harper

TV Personality

It is never worth it to hold a grudge.
It only makes you feel bad.

Dr. Susan Love

President, Dr. Susan Love Research Foundation

5 NOVEMBER

Write it down.

Nancy McFadden

Senior Vice President and
Senior Advisor to the Chairman
and CEO, PG&E Corporation

6 NOVEMBER

In a "New Rules" environment you not only get to create freely, you get to develop a brand new paradigm. So, what are you waiting for?

SONIA ALLEYNE

Editorial Director, Black Enterprise

7 NOVEMBER

There is no object in your home
more important than the people in it.

Alice Domar

Director, Domar Center for Mind/Body Health,
Co-Author, Live a Little, Expert, BeWell.com

Always, always, always have your own money. You just never know.

LISA LING

Journalist

9 NOVEMBER

There are three ingredients that turn a woman into a siren: Lashes, push-up bra and a rockin' pair of heels.

Jeannie Mai

Host, How Do I Look? The Style Network

10 NOVEMBER

Live outside your comfort zone,
there are great discoveries there.

Caroline Aaron
Actress, Writer

11 NOVEMBER

The moment you judge someone
you lose the power to influence them
in a significant and ongoing way.

Tony Robbins

Entrepreneur, Author, Peak Performance Strategist

12 NOVEMBER

Know your friends and keep them close.
Your friends and family are the most precious
of possessions.

Judy Woodruff
Senior Correspondent, The PBS NewsHour

13 NOVEMBER

There is no doubt that the battle of the sexes is taking on a new meaning, where expectations and responsibilities have to be re-examined.

MARIA ELENA SALINAS

Univision News Anchor

14 NOVEMBER

A great mentor challenges you to be better than you are— and better than they are.

Christine Dahm

Vice President, Marketing,
Nestlé Prepared Foods Company

15 NOVEMBER

Learn how to drive a stick shift.

Eve Ensler
Playwright, Performer, Activist

We don't just feed people—we nurture their human dignity.

Betty Chinn

*Founder, Betty's Angels,
2008 Minerva Award® Recipient*

17 NOVEMBER

My grandmother said, "Silence is the sound of money talking." Never pass up the opportunity to break that kind of silence.

SANDRA STEINGRABER

Acclaimed Ecologist, Author, Survivor

You can do anything you want
but you have to have a plan.

Luong Ung

Activist, Author, Lecturer

19 NOVEMBER

Travel and aim to see the world.
You'll gain clarity on your own life.

NICHOLAS KRISTOF

Columnist, New York Times

20 NOVEMBER

If you are creating a campaign
for change, always begin by thinking
how you would react if you
were on the receiving end.

Molly Melching

Executive Director, Tostan

21 NOVEMBER

Create a sturdy foundation upon which to build your life.

Tracee Ellis Ross

Actress, Mentor, Teen Advocate

Think a level above.
Make decisions as if
you were your manager.

Lisa Stevens

EVP, Regional President,
California Regional Banking,
Wells Fargo & Company

23 NOVEMBER

Passion, a plan and practice are critical elements to success.

Laila Ali

World Champion Athlete,
Television Personality, Mother

24 NOVEMBER

Being a parent is the toughest job in the world and there's no school you can go to for it.

PETER GALLAGHER

Actor

25 NOVEMBER

Ask for what you want and need.

Billie Jean King

Co-Founder, World TeamTennis, Wimbledon Champion,
Founder, Women's Sports Foundation
2009 Minerva Award® Recipient

If we let our egos run wild,
it only makes this already
troubled world worse.

Shinjo Ito
Founder of Shinnyo-en

27 NOVEMBER

As women, we've been discussing everything from sex to diets for decades. It's time to start talking about money.

Alexa von Tobel

Founder, CEO, LearnVest Inc.

28 NOVEMBER

Take the breath that it takes to complain and hold it in your lungs until that breath turns to an air of change.

AZURE ANTOINETTE

Poet, Spoken Word Artist

29 NOVEMBER

Exceptional dreamers genuinely touch people's lives.

Marilyn Hamilton

Founder, Winners on Wheels,
2006 Minerva Award® Recipient

30 NOVEMBER

As the father of two daughters,
it will eventually be "time."
God help me!

DAYMOND JOHN

CEO, FUBU The Collection,
Branding Expert, Author

1 DECEMBER

Strength doesn't have to be internal, it can come from the support of those whose shoulders you are standing on.

Jacy Good

FocusDriven Board Member

Empowering women means empowering the world, let's do it!

Graciela Meibar

Vice President Global Diversity, Mattel, Inc.

3 DECEMBER

It is totally permissible to occasionally take a long hard look in the mirror and in a truthful and objective fashion proclaim, "I am the shit."

Rosario Dawson

Actress, Co-Founder, Voto Latino

4 DECEMBER

It is in your moments
of decision that your
destiny is shaped.

Tony Robbins

*Entrepreneur, Author,
Peak Performance Strategist*

5 DECEMBER

When it's time to do something scary, do it scared. Wait until fear spontaneously vanishes and you'll wait forever.

MARTHA BECK

Author/Life Coach

6 DECEMBER

Luck is over-rated.
Persistence is what pays.

Buddy Valastro

Owner, Carlo's Bakery aka The Cake Boss

7 DECEMBER

Refuse to let self doubt, age, odds, timing and circumstance convince you your dream is not possible. Dig deep to slay the doubt, the demons, the darkness and go for your dream!

Giselle Fernandez
President, F Squared Enterprises

At least once a day pause and repeat: "I totally and completely love and accept myself."

Louann Brizendine, M.D.

New York Times Best-Selling Author, The Female Brain & The Male Brain

9 DECEMBER

The first step is overcoming the pull of the living room couch.

EDIT SCHLAFFER

Founder, Women without Borders,
SAVE - Sisters Against Violent Extremism

Contrary to movie lore, you can't just sit on your couch and imagine checks coming into your mailbox. You must get off your butt and ACT.

Darren Hardy

Publisher and Editorial Director, SUCCESS

11 DECEMBER

People ask me why small women can often climb better than big burly men. I tell them, finesse gets you farther than strength every time.

TERESA DELFIN

Founder, Mountain Mama, Inc.

12 DECEMBER

Love yourself and you can heal your life.

Louise Hay

Author, You Can Heal Your Life and Founder of Hay House Publishing, 2008 Minerva Award® Recipient

13 DECEMBER

It's amazing what you can do when you stop worrying about failing.

Anne Sweeney

Co-chair, Disney Media Networks,
President, Disney/ABC Television Group

The days are long
but the years are short.

Gretchen Rubin

Writer, The Happiness Project

15 DECEMBER

Time is like make-up.
The more you need it,
the less it can do for you.

Linda Ellerbee

*Television Producer, Journalist,
Best-Selling Author*

When you set out to achieve your goal, stay intensely focused. Do not allow anyone or any situation to stray your course.

DAVID GOLDMAN

Devoted Father

17 DECEMBER

Start each day by asking,
"What will I do today to make
it better than yesterday?"

Tory Johnson

CEO, Women For Hire;
Workplace Contributor, Good Morning America

Speed up.

Kristin Perry

*Plaintiff, Perry v.
Schwarzenegger*

19 DECEMBER

Stick to the fight when you're hardest hit. It's when things seem worst that you mustn't quit!

Jake Steinfeld

Chairman and CEO of Body by Jake Global

20 DECEMBER

"Fail fast-forward." Don't be afraid to fail.
If you do, identify it and move ahead quickly
so momentum isn't lost.

CAROL BARTZ

CEO, Yahoo! Inc.

21 DECEMBER

It's time to smile!

Giada De Laurentiis

Celebrity Chef, #1 New York Times'
Best-Selling Cookbook Author

Accept and embrace responsibility.

TAMI ERWIN

President, West Area, Verizon Wireless

23 DECEMBER

Never leave home without powder and lipstick. They cover a multitude of sins.

Deborah Roberts

ABC News Correspondent

You are entitled to the dignity
of your own experience.

Natasha Lyonne

Actress

25 DECEMBER

Wake up every day knowing you have the power. Understanding the big picture is understanding small wins. Make every moment count.

Rodney Peete

Sports Star, TV/Radio Personality, Author, Philanthropist

Do not let your silence become an accomplice of evil.

Claudia Julie Duque

Journalist, IWMF Courage in Journalism Award Winner 2010

27 DECEMBER

Sometimes an expletive really is the best word to describe a challenging situation.

KATHY HULL

Founder, The George Mark Children's House, 2009 Minerva Award® Recipient

Do the right thing.

Leslie Dance

*Director and Vice President of
Brand Marketing and Communications,
Eastman Kodak Company*

29 DECEMBER

I know I might fall trying new things but I refuse to let that stop me from discovering what is possible.

Kristina Ripatti

Retired LAPD Officer

30 DECEMBER

Never compare your insides
to someone else's outsides.

Rob Lowe

Actor, Producer, Entrepreneur

31 DECEMBER

Three words to live by: Pass it on.

MARIA SHRIVER

First Lady of California

Index *of* Quotes

A

Aaron, Caroline—*Mar 19, May 20, Nov 10*

Ali, Laila—*Feb 27, May 27, Nov 23*

Alleyne, Sonia—*Mar 1, Jul 22, Nov 6*

Antoinette, Azure—*Apr 21, Sep 11, Nov 28*

Ashby, Crystal—*Mar 12, Aug 18, Oct 17*

B

Barnouin, Kim—*Mar 20, Oct 19*

Bartz, Carol—*Mar 11, Sep 1, Dec 20*

Beck, Martha—*Jan 14, Aug 9, Dec 5*

Blashek, Carolyn—*Feb 5, Jun 28, Sep 17*

Boston, Lloyd—*Apr 26, Jul 19, Oct 10*

Brizendine, Louann—*Feb 16, Aug 10, Dec 8*

Brockovich, Erin—*Apr 4, Jun 26, Oct 9*

Brown, Campbell—*Mar 7, Jun 6, Oct 18*

Brown, Dr. Helene—*Sep 8*

Brown, Jerry—*Jan 22*

Brown, Oral Lee—*Mar 2, Jul 25, Oct 5*

Bush, Laura—*Jan 9, Jul 26, Oct 2*

C

Chang, Juju—*Apr 8, Aug 19, Sep 26*

Chinn, Betty—*Nov 16*

Chopra, Deepak—*Jan 18, Jul 17, Sep 18*

Christie, Blair—*May 13, Jun 4, Oct 4*

Claudia, Julie Duque—*Feb 20*

Cora, Cat—*Jan 28, Apr 22, Jun 24*

D

Dahm, Christine—*Apr 5, Sep 4, Nov 14*

Dance, Leslie—*Feb 15, Jun 30, Dec 28*

Dawson, Rosario—*Feb 1, Sep 16, Dec 3*

De Laurentiis, Giada—*Jan 23, Aug 31, Dec 21*

Deen, Paula—*Jan 17, Jun 12, Oct 6*

DeFrantz, Anita—*Jul 7*

Delfin, Teresa—*Mar 29, Jul 27, Dec 11*

Denzel, Nora—*Mar 25, Sep 9, 21*

Dodge, Sister Terry—*Mar 30, Jun 15, Oct 20*

Domar, Alice—*Apr 27, Jun 18, Nov 7*

Duque, Claudia Julie—*Aug 21, Dec 26*

E

Ellerbee, Linda—*Feb 17, Jun 2, Dec 15*

Ensler, Eve—*Jan 30, Jul 13, Nov 15*

Epstein, Dr. Robert—*Apr 9, Jul 29, Oct 16*

Erwin, Tami—*Apr 18, Aug 24, Dec 22*

F

Fernandez, Giselle—*Jan 9, Mar 14, Jun 5, Dec 7*

Field, Sally—*Feb 22, Jun 29, Nov 2*

Fona, Jane—*Jan 16, Aug 26*

Frye, Soleil Moon—*May 2, Jul 15*

G

Gallagher, Peter—*Mar 8, Sep 2, Nov 24*

Gibbons, Leeza—*Feb 2, May 28, Sep 19*

Gibbs, Kristin—*Apr 3*

Gin, Jennie Hernandez—*Apr 28*

Ginsburg, Ruth Bader—*Jan 4, Feb 10, Jun 14, Nov 1*

Goldman, David—*Apr 14, Aug 22, Dec 16*

Good, Jacy—*Apr 10, Jul 2, Dec 1*

Goodall, Jane—*Feb 23*

H

Hamilton, Marilyn—*Nov 29*

Hardy, Darren—*Feb 19, Jul 12, Dec 10*

Harper, Bob—*May 4, Sep 5, Nov 3*

Harris, Alice—*May 19*

Hawn, Goldie—*Feb 3, Jul 20, Sep 14*

Hay, Louise—*Dec 12*

Hull, Kathy—*Dec 27*

I

Ito, Shinjo—*Feb 24, Jun 11, Nov 26*

J

John, Daymond—*Mar 22, May 30, Nov 30*

Johnson, Betsy—*Mar 31, Jul 30, Oct 29*

Johnson, Rafer—*Apr 17, Sep 10*

Johnson, Tory—*Apr 29, Jul 3, Dec 17*

K

Kane, Carol—*Feb 18*

Karan, Donna—*May 15, Jul 4, Oct 14*

Kennedy, Caroline—*Mar 9, May 24*

King, Billie Jean—*Mar 10, Aug 17, Nov 25*

King, Gayle—*Feb 12, Jun 10, Jul 5, Oct 15*

Knight, Phil—*Jan 20*

Kristof, Nicholas—*Feb 9, Jun 7, Nov 19*

L

Lechtenberg, Sister Jennie—*Apr 15*

Lesser, Elizabeth—*Feb 11, Jun 16, Sep 13*

Ling, Laura—*May 6, Jun 8, Oct 13*

Ling, Lisa—*Feb 25, Jul 31, Nov 8*

Love, Dr. Susan—*Mar 17, May 23, Nov 4*

Lowe, Rob—*Feb 13, Jul 24, Dec 30*

Lyonne, Natasha—*Apr 25, Aug 6, Dec 24*

M

Maas, David and Dania—*Apr 2, Jun 17, Sep 23*

Mai, Jeannie—*May 9, Aug 1, Nov 9*

Margaritis, William—*Mar 18, Jun 22, Sep 28*

Markovits, Ivelise — *Sep 30*

McCain, Meghan — *Mar 16, Oct 31*

McFadden, Nancy — *Apr 11, Jul 23, Nov 5*

Meibar, Graciela — *May 18, Aug 11, Dec 2*

Melching, Molly — *May 17, Jun 23, Nov 20*

Michaels, Jillian — *Jan 13, May 29, Sep 20*

Miller, Jan — Mar 3, *Jun 21*

Mirikitani, Janice — *Feb 14*

Mulcahy, Anne — *May 12, Jul 16, Oct 21*

N

Nilan, Mary Ann Wasil — *Apr 19, Jun 25, Oct 27*

O

Obama, Michelle — *Jan 2, Mar 26, Aug 23*

O'Brien, Kathy — *Jul 5, Oct 30*

O'Conner, Sandra Day — *Jan 6*

Oliver, Mary — *Jan 8, Aug 5, Oct 8*

Orman, Suze — *Jan 11, Aug 12, Sep 27*

Oz, Dr. Mehmet — *Jan 15, May 21*

Oz, Lisa—*Apr 12, Aug 27, Oct 28*

Oz, Mehmet—*Oct 3*

P

Peete Rodney—*Apr 24*

Peete, Holly Robinson—*Apr 7, Jul 28, Oct 23*

Peete, Rodney—*Jul 1, Dec 25*

Pennington, Maureen—*Jun 13*

Perry, Kristin—*Mar 23, Sep 6, Dec 18*

Porter, Christy—*Aug 4*

R

Redford, Robert—*Jan 12*

Renda, Larree—*Jan 27, May 25, Sep 15*

Ride, Dr. Sally—*Mar 5*

Ripatti, Kristina—*Apr 6, Aug 2, Dec 29*

Robbins, Tony—*Jan 24, Aug 8, Nov 11, Dec 4*

Roberts, Deborah—*May 3, Aug 7, Dec 23*

Roberts, Robin—*May 1*

Roker, Al—*Jan 29, Aug 28*

Ross, Tracee Ellis—*Feb 6, Jun 20, Nov 21*

Rubenstein, Hal—*Mar 27, Oct 7*

Rubin, Gretchen—*Apr 16, Jul 21, Dec 14*

S

Salinas, Maria Elena—*Mar 4, May 31, Nov 13*

Savard, Dr. Marie—*Jan 31, May 26, Sep 24*

Sawyer, Diane—*Jan 5*

Schlaffer, Edit—*May 10, Aug 13, Dec 9*

Schori, Dr. Katharine Jefferts—*Apr 23, Jul 18, Sep 22*

Schultz, Howard—*Jan 26*

Schwarzenegger, Arnold—*Jan 7, Jul 8, Oct 24*

Schwarzenegger, Katherine—*Mar 13, Jun 19, Sep 12*

Sheehy, Gail—*Jan 10, Mar 21, Aug 14*

Shriver, Eunice Kennedy—*Jan 19, Sep 25*

Shriver, Maria—*Jan 1, Jun 3, Sep 29, Dec 31*

Silbert, Mimi—*Aug 25*

Simpson, Jessica—*Jan 25, Aug 16, Oct 26*

Steinem, Gloria—*Oct 22*

Steinfeld, Jake—*May 11, Aug 15, Dec 19*

Steingraber, Sandra—*Apr 13, Sep 7, Nov 17*

Stevens, Agnes—*Mar 24*

Stevens, Lisa—*Mar 6, Jun 1, Nov 22*

Stier, Sandra—*May 14, Jul 10, Oct 12*

Sweeney, Anne—*Feb 21, Jul 11, Dec 13*

T

Tousi, Susan—*Feb 8*

U

Ung, Luong—*May 5, Aug 29, Nov 18*

V

Valastro, Buddy—*Feb 26, Aug 3, Dec 6*

Vivio, Lavern—*May 16*

von Tobel, Alexa—*Apr 30, Nov 27*

W

Ward, Laysha—*Jan 21, Aug 30, Oct 25*

Washington, Lula—*Feb 28*

Waukazoo, Helen—*May 8*

Weiner, Jess—*Apr 1*

Wentworth, Alexandra—*Mar 28, Jul 14, Oct 1*

White, James D.—*Feb 4, Jun 27*

Williams, Brian—*Feb 7*

Wilson, Rita—*Apr 20, Sep 3, Oct 11*

Winfrey, Oprah—*Jan 3, Mar 15, May 22, Aug 20*

Woodruff, Judy—*May 7, Jul 9, Nov 12*